Monarch Mystery

Daniel Shepard
Illustrated by Dan Grant

Rigby®

A Harcourt Achieve Imprint

www.Rigby.com
1-800-531-5015

One day the teacher showed a plant to the class. "What is that?" asked Sarah.

"It's a milkweed plant,"
said the teacher.

3

"What is that?"
asked Sarah.

"That is an egg from a monarch butterfly," said the teacher.

milkweed

plant bug

5

The teacher put the plant in a safe place.

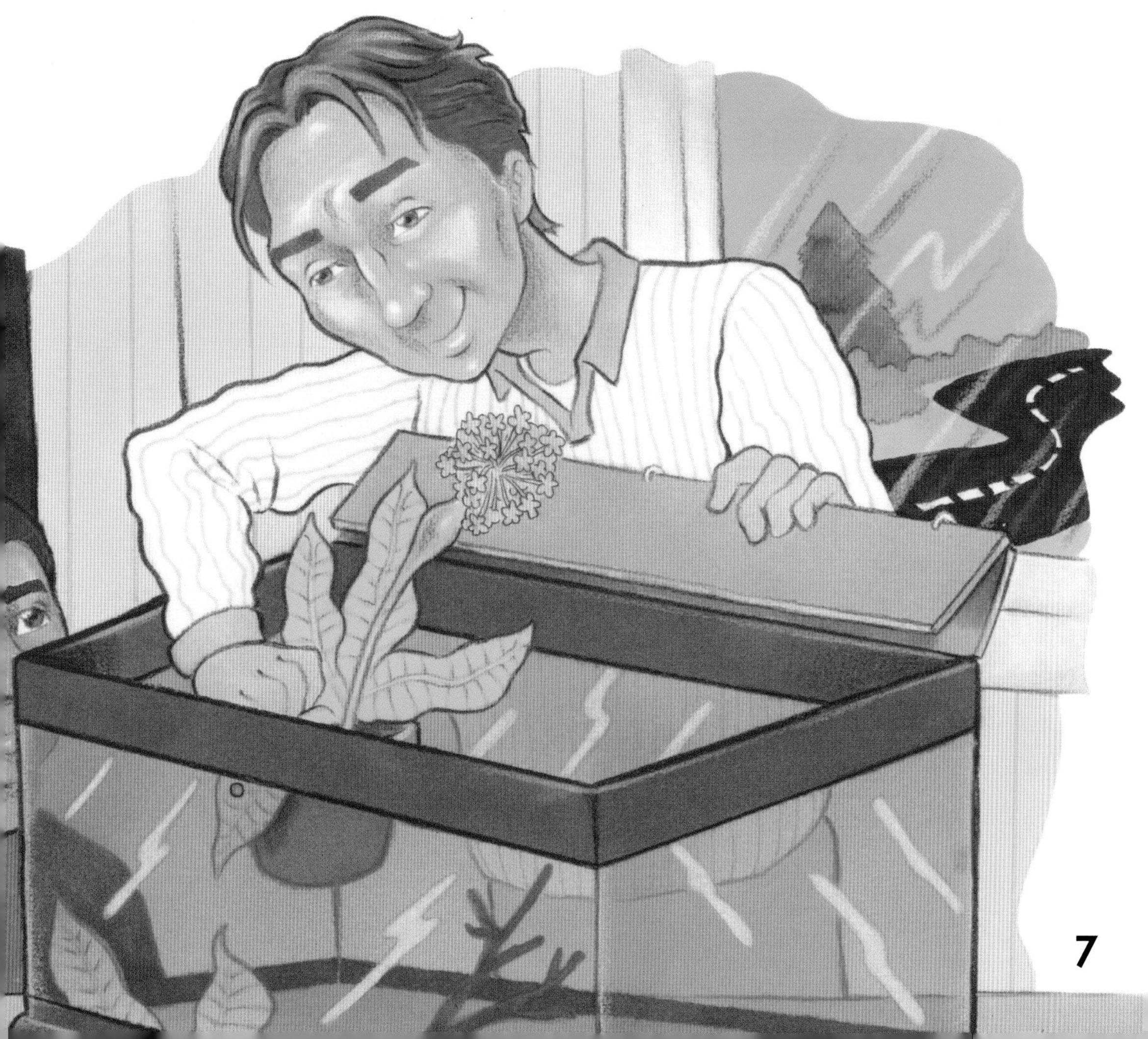

"What is that?"
asked Sarah.

"That is a caterpillar,"
said the teacher.

The caterpillar ate
the milkweed.

The caterpillar grew.

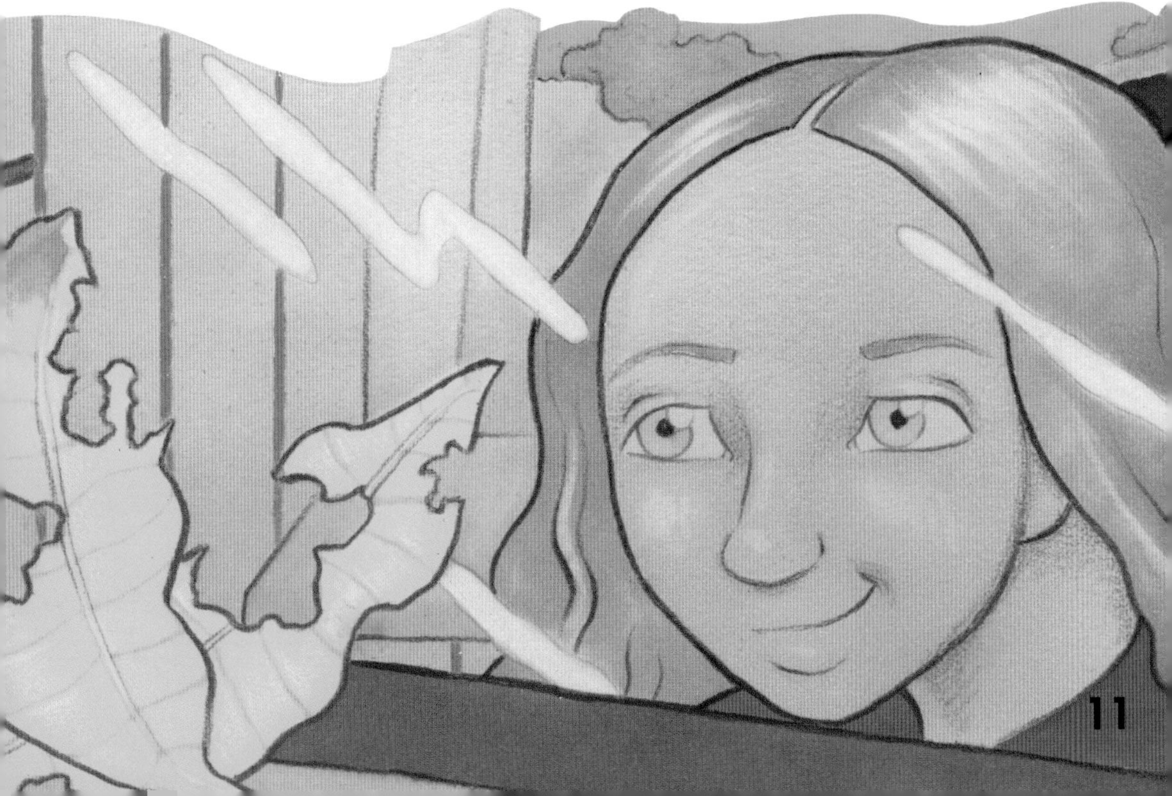

"What is that?"
asked Sarah.
"That is a pupa,"
said the teacher.
"The caterpillar is inside.
Soon it will be a butterfly."

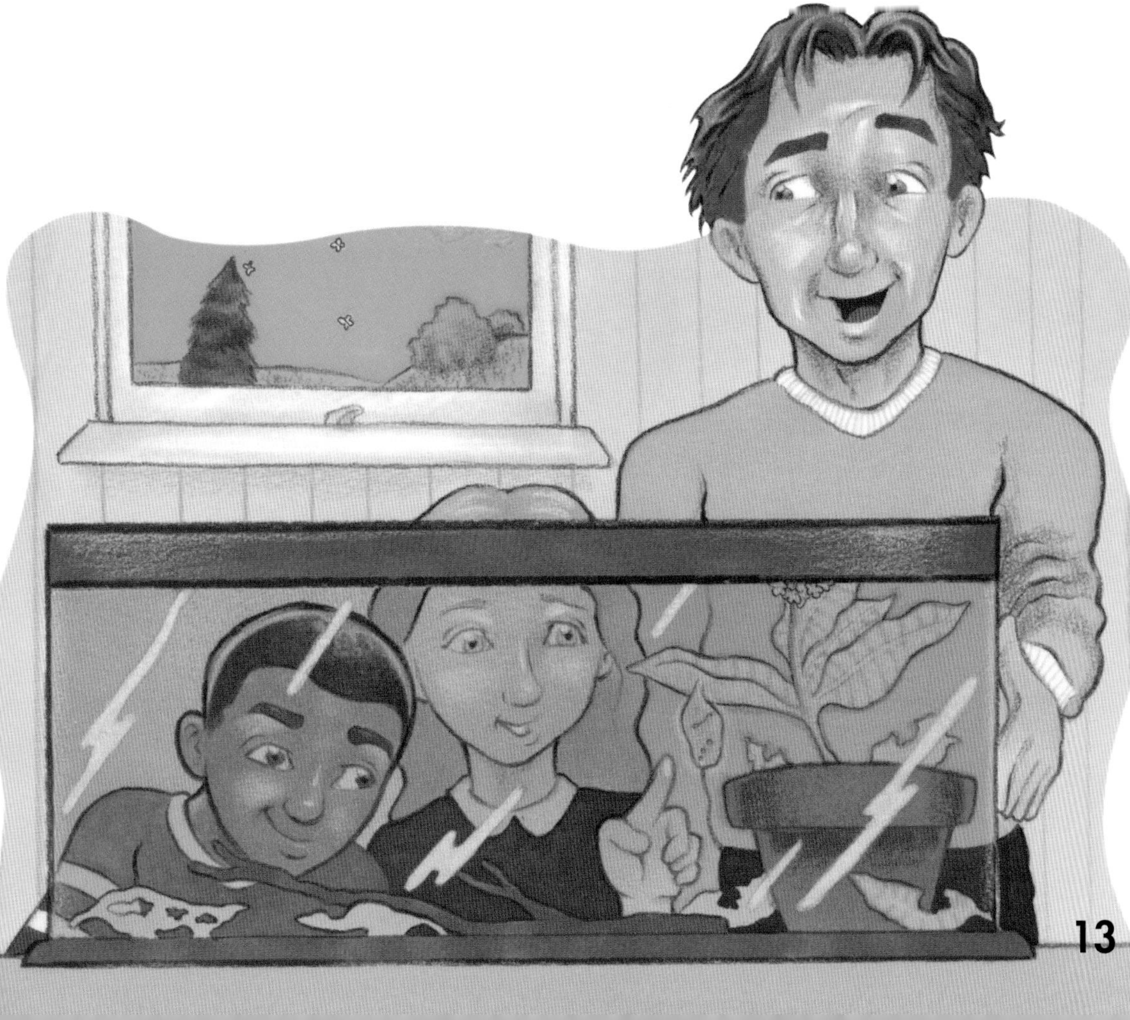

The monarch butterfly came out one day.

"Some monarchs fly to Mexico," said the teacher.

"How do they know where to go?" asked Sarah. "That is the monarch mystery," said the teacher.

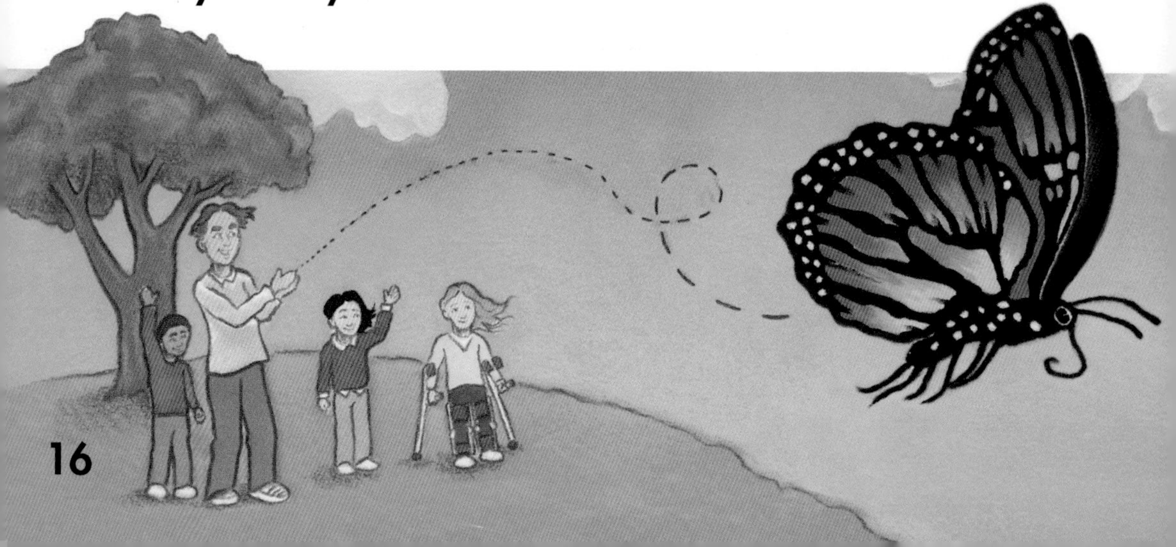